# Picture postcards of
# Prince Charles
## and his family.

Compiled by Mary Dunkin

**Omnibus Press**
London/New York/Sydney

60P

*(The numerals in these captions refer to the figures in the lower left-hand corner on the back of each postcard).*

Prince Charles was born on 14th November, 1948 **1, 2, 3, 4** and the following December was christened Charles Philip Arthur George in the Music Room at Buckingham Palace. Here he is after the ceremony with **1, 3** Princess Elizabeth **2** Princess Elizabeth and the Duke of Edinburgh and **4** the Queen. Photographs by Baron, the well-known society photographer.

**5, 6, 7, 9, 10** Prince Charles at 19 weeks old.

**8, 11, 12** Prince Charles' first birthday photographs.

**13** The first photograph of Prince Charles with his sister Princess Anne, taken by Cecil Beaton in September 1950, a month after she was born and **14** with Princess Elizabeth.

**15, 16** Members of the Royal Family at Princess Anne's christening on 21st October 1950.

**17, 23, 24** Informal photographs taken in the grounds of Balmoral Castle on the occasion of Prince Charles' fourth birthday. **18** Four-year old Prince Charles acknowledges the crowds after the first State Opening of Parliament of the Queen's reign.

**19** The Royal Family in the garden of their home, Clarence House, in August 1951.

**20, 26, 38** Portraits by Marcus Adams taken when the Prince was four years old.

**21** Two-year old Prince Charles and his family taken at Clarence House.

**22** After the Trooping the Colour ceremony in 1953.

**25, 27, 28** Portraits by Marcus Adams taken when the prince was three.

**29, 32** The Queen, Prince Charles, Princess Anne and Prince Philip after the Coronation ceremony in June 1953.

**31** King George VI chats to Prince Charles while the Queen holds Princess Anne. It was on the occasion of Prince Charles' third birthday and only a few months before the King died.

**30** The Queen, Princess Anne and Prince Charles acknowledge the crowds after the Queen's return from her Commonwealth tour of 1954.

**34, 36** The Royal Family in the grounds of Balmoral Castle during their summer holiday, in August 1955.

**33** Princess Anne and Prince Charles, watched by the Queen, playing on a see-saw which they found in the grounds of a saw-mill on the Balmoral estate and **35** on the dairy farm on the estate, in August 1957, with their parents.

**37** A Marcus Adams portrait taken in 1954.

**39** Princess Anne and Prince Charles in the grounds of Royal Lodge, Windsor in April 1954.

**40** On the occasion of the Princess's third birthday. They are both wearing the clothes which they wore on Coronation Day. The Princess's dress is of cream French lace over chiffon and taffeta. Prince Charles is wearing cream serge trousers with a cream spun silk shirt.

**41** Drawn by A.K. Lawrence at Windsor Castle in April 1957.

**42** Princess Anne and Prince Charles arrive at a London station.

**43** The Prince returning to Cheam School after attending morning service, in July 1958. On the previous day the Queen had announced her intention to create him Prince of Wales.

**44, 47** The Royal Family in the grounds of Windsor Castle in June 1959. In **44** Sugar, the Queen's corgi, lies in the foreground.

**45, 46, 48** Informal photographs of the Royal Family with the seven-month old Prince Andrew taken during their summer holiday at Balmoral in 1960 **50** With his sister and brothers at Balmoral.

**49, 52, 53** The Royal Family with the Queen's youngest son, one-year old Prince Edward in the grounds of Frogmore.

**51** In the grounds of Windsor Castle in April 1962, shortly before Prince Charles went to Gordonstoun. Prince Andrew is standing between Prince Philip and the Queen.

**54** At Frogmore in April 1968.

**55** Family Group at Madame Tussaud's.

**56** A detail from a portrait by John Hughes Hallett painted in 1972. The painting was commissioned by R.A.F. Strike Command and hangs in their Officers Mess in High Wycombe.

**57** Prince Charles taking the salute when he presented Colours to a Welsh Army Unit in Cardiff, in 1969.

**58, 59, 60** Three postcards produced to celebrate the Investiture of H.R.H. The Prince of Wales on July 1st 1969.

**61** A formal portrait taken after the Investiture by Norman Parkinson.

**62, 63** The Prince after he was installed as a Knight of the Most Noble Order of the Garter in June 1968.

**64** At Garter installation ceremony in June 1972.

**65, 66, 67, 68** Four photographs taken by Peter Grugeon in the Grand Hall of Windsor Castle, to commemorate the Prince's official tour of America and Canada in 1977. In the uniforms of **65** Commander in the Royal Navy **66** Wing Commander in the Royal Air Force **67** Colonel-in-Chief of the Royal Regiment of Wales **68** Colonel of the Welsh Guards.

**69** An informal photograph taken during the filming of a BBC documentary on the Royal Family.

**70** A portrait by Carole Cutner taken in 1974.

**71, 72** Two informal photographs by Karsh of Ottawa, taken at the residence of the Governor General of Canada in Ottawa during the Prince's visit in 1975.

**73** Captain Mark Phillips, Princess Anne, the Queen Mother, the Queen, Prince Charles, Prince Andrew, Prince Philip and Lady Sarah Armstrong-Jones taken at Sandringham in January 1977 during the Christmas holiday.

**74, 79, 80** On February 24th 1981 Prince Charles' engagement to Lady Diana Spencer was announced. Here the couple are photographed at Buckingham Palace. Lady Diana's engagement ring, made by Garrards, is an oval sapphire surrounded by fourteen diamonds and set in 18 carat white gold.

**74** The Royal Family group photograph taken on the Queen Mother's 80th birthday.

**75** A composite postcard with portraits of Prince Charles in 1969, the Queen and Prince Philip in 1965, and Princess Anne, Prince Edward and Prince Andrew in 1968.

**76** Princess Anne, Captain Mark Phillips, Prince Philip, the Queen, Lord Mountbatten, Prince Andrew, Prince Edward and Prince Charles wave to the crowds from the balcony of Buckingham Palace after the Queen's Silver Jubilee Thanksgiving Service in June 1977.

**77** Prince Charles during his visit to India in 1980.

**78** Prince Charles on his 30th birthday in the grounds of Balmoral Castle.

**Copyright holders of photographs** Associated Press: 57. Camera Press: 1, 2, 3, 4, 5, 6, 7, 8, 9, 10, 11, 12, 13, 15, 16, 20, 21, 38, 58, 60, 61, 63, 65, 66, 67, 68, 71, 72, 75, 78, 80. Fox Photos: 74, 79. Hulton Picture Library: 17, 24, 39. Keystone: 19, 29, 30, 34, 36, 44, 45, 46, 47, 48, 76. Madame Tussauds: 55. Press Association: 43, 49, 54. Tim Graham: 77. Times: 23.

We thank the following for their kind co-operation in the production of this book – J. Arthur Dixon, Jarrold and Sons, Judges, Pitkin Pictorial, Photo Precision Ltd., J. Salmon, Charles Skilton, and Raphael Tuck.

Editor/Art Director: Pearce Marchbank. Production: Robert Sampson. Origination by East Anglian Engravers, Norwich.
Printed and bound by William Clowes (Beccles) Limited, England. Board Supplied by A.H. James & Co. Limited, London.

## Omnibus Press

(A division of Book Sales Limited)
Published in 1981
Copyright © 1981 by Mary Dunkin
Distributed by
Book Sales Limited, 78 Newman Street, London W1P 3LA.
Book Sales Pty. Limited, 27 Clarendon Street, Artarmon, Sydney, NSW 2064, Australia.

PRINCESS ELIZABETH WITH HER INFANT SON PRINCE CHARLES

H.R.H. PRINCESS ELIZABETH AND H.R.H. THE DUKE OF EDINBURGH
WITH THE INFANT PRINCE CHARLES

H.R.H. PRINCESS ELIZABETH WITH HER INFANT SON PRINCE CHARLES

HER MAJESTY THE QUEEN WITH THE INFANT PRINCE CHARLES

POST CARD

POST CARD

Photochrom Company Limited
Graphic Studios, Tunbridge Wells, Kent
2

TUCK'S POST CARD

CARTE    POSTALE

FOR ADDRESS ONLY

THE WORLDS ART SERVICE
RAPHAEL TUCK & SONS

BY APPOINTMENT
FINE ART PUBLISHERS

TRADE MARK

Printed in England

FINE ART PUBLISHERS TO THEIR MAJESTIES THE KING & QUEEN AND TO HER MAJESTY QUEEN MARY

Raphael Tuck & Sons Ltd          REAL PHOTOGRAPH
1

POST CARD

Photochrom Company Limited
Graphic Studios, Tunbridge Wells, Kent
4

POST CARD

Photochrom Company Limited
Graphic Studios, Tunbridge Wells, Kent
3

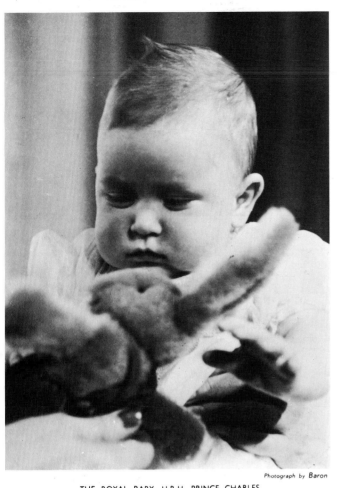

THE ROYAL BABY, H.R.H. PRINCE CHARLES

*Photograph by Baron*

THE ROYAL BABY, H.R.H. PRINCE CHARLES

*Photograph by Baron*

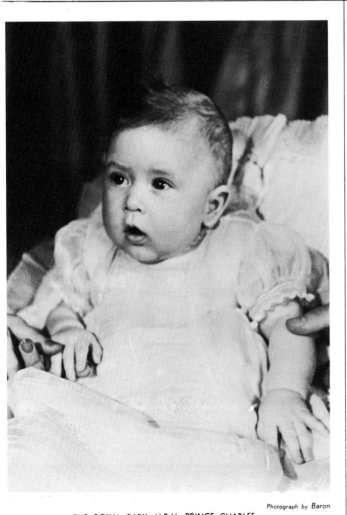

*Photograph by Baron*

THE ROYAL BABY, H.R.H. PRINCE CHARLES

THE ROYAL BABY, H.R.H. PRINCE CHARLES

*From a Portrait by Marcus Adams*

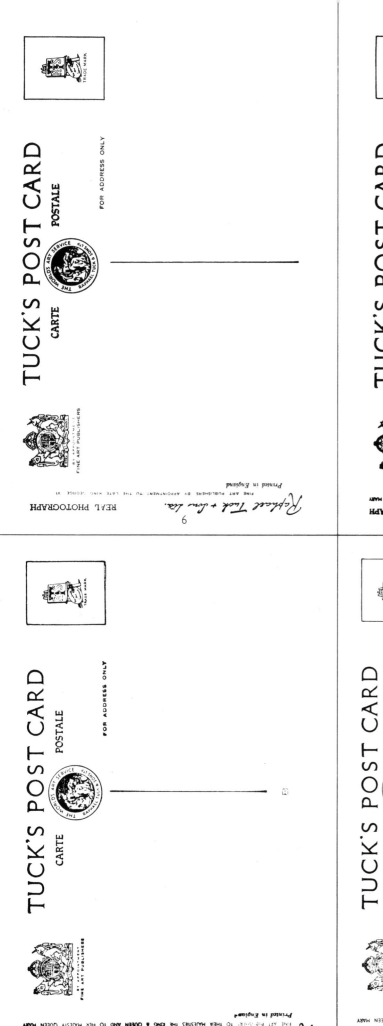

T.R.H. THE DUKE AND DUCHESS OF EDINBURGH
AND H.R.H. PRINCE CHARLES

H.R.H. PRINCESS ELIZABETH AND PRINCE CHARLES

H.R.H. PRINCESS ELIZABETH AND PRINCE CHARLES

H.R.H. PRINCESS ELIZABETH AND PRINCE CHARLES

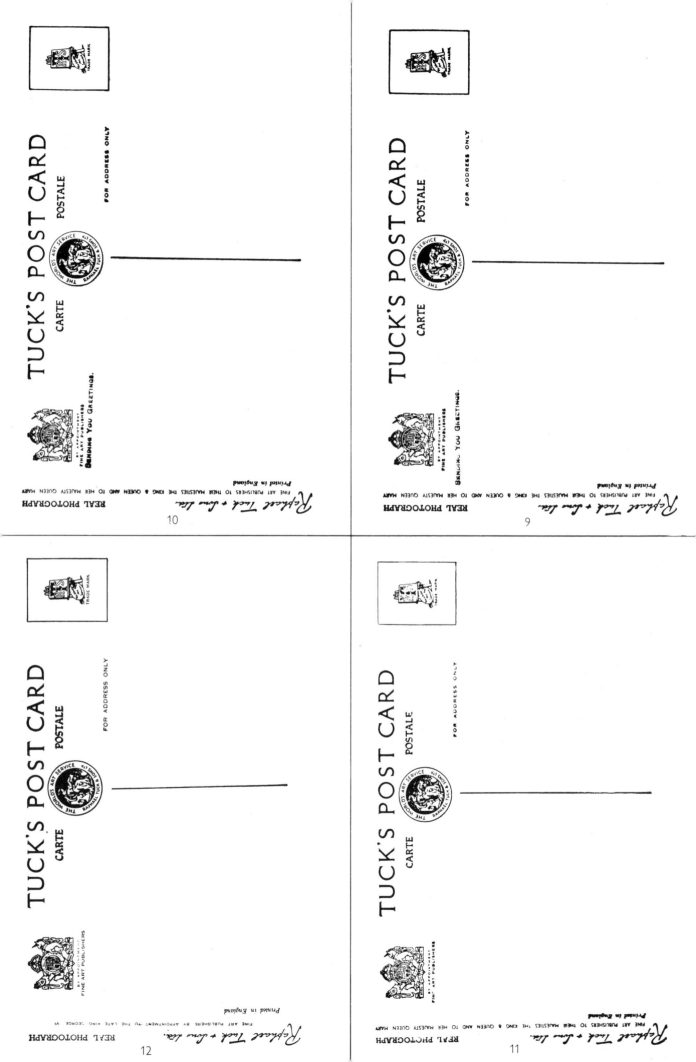

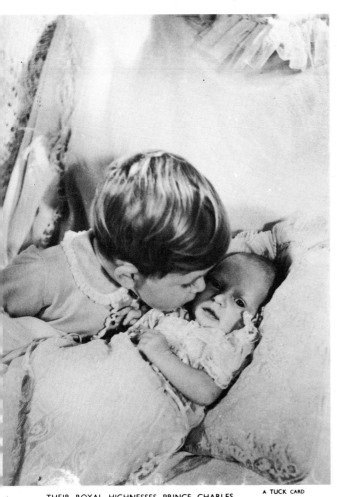

THEIR ROYAL HIGHNESSES PRINCE CHARLES
AND PRINCESS ANNE

A TUCK CARD

HER ROYAL HIGHNESS PRINCESS ELIZABETH WITH
PRINCE CHARLES AND PRINCESS ANNE

89c

Baron

H.M. THE QUEEN, T.R.H. THE DUKE AND DUCHESS OF EDINBURGH,
PRINCE CHARLES AND PRINCESS ANNE

89d

Baron

H.M. THE QUEEN WITH PRINCE CHARLES

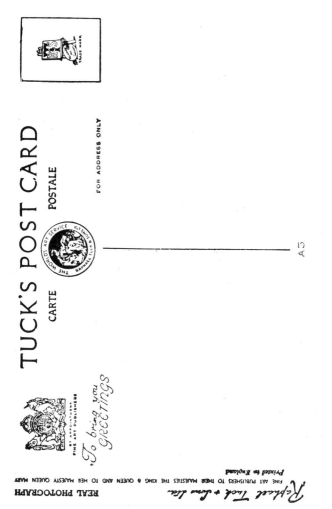

14

13

16

15

Photo Studio Lisa

H.M. Queen Elizabeth II with T.R.H. Prince Charles & Princess Anne

THE ROYAL FAMILY ON THE BALCONY, BUCKINGHAM PALACE.

A TUCK CARD

T.R.H. THE DUKE AND DUCHESS OF EDINBURGH
WITH PRINCE CHARLES AND PRINCESS ANNE

98 B

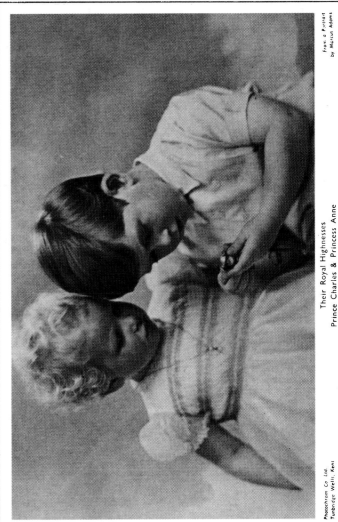

From a Portrait
by Marcus Adams

Their Royal Highnesses
Prince Charles & Princess Anne

Photochrom Co Ltd.
Tunbridge Wells, Kent

SENDING YOU GREETINGS

POST CARD

*Valentine's*

FOR ADDRESS ONLY

E.R. 17

— THIS IS A REAL PHOTOGRAPH —

PRINTED IN
GT BRITAIN

M

18

*Photochrom*

Greetings

POST CARD

*Publishers to the World*

for address only

17

*Photochrom*

Greetings

POST CARD

*Publishers to the World*

for address only

20

REAL PHOTOGRAPH

Greetings
to You

BY APPOINTMENT
FINE ART PUBLISHERS

TUCK'S POST CARD

CARTE POSTALE

FOR ADDRESS ONLY

19

7K                                *Karsh of Ottawa*

**H.M. QUEEN ELIZABETH II
H.R.H. PRINCE CHARLES, H.R.H. PRINCESS ANNE
H.R.H. THE DUKE OF EDINBURGH**

TC 16                                A TUCK CARD

THE DUKE OF EDINBURGH AND PRINCE CHARLES ON THE BALCONY
OF BUCKINGHAM PALACE AFTER THE TROOPING THE
COLOUR CEREMONY

THE ROYAL FAMILY AT BALMORAL.     "TIMES PHOTOGRAPH"

Photochrom Co. Ltd.,
Tunbridge Wells, Kent.          Photo Studio Lisa

H.M. Queen Elizabeth II
& her children

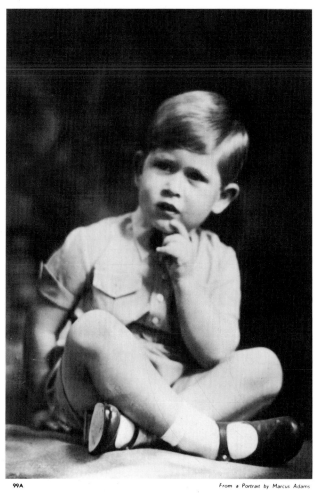

99A                         From a Portrait by Marcus Adams

HIS ROYAL HIGHNESS PRINCE CHARLES

H.R.H. PRINCE CHARLES, DUKE OF CORNWALL.
PHOTO BY MARCUS ADAMS.                   701

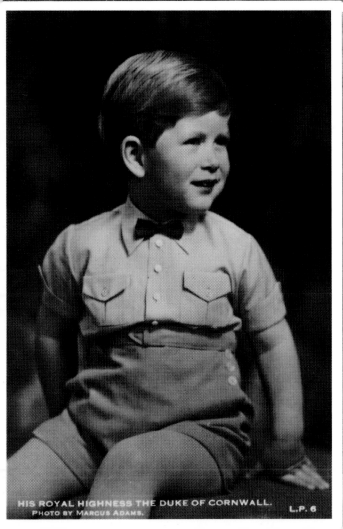

HIS ROYAL HIGHNESS THE DUKE OF CORNWALL.
PHOTO BY MARCUS ADAMS.              L.P. 6

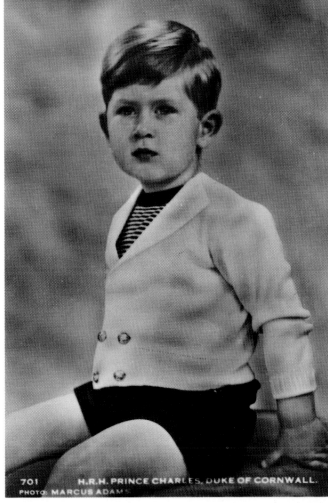

701        H.R.H. PRINCE CHARLES, DUKE OF CORNWALL.
PHOTO: MARCUS ADAMS.

## 26

POST CARD

PRINTED IN ENGLAND

THIS SPACE FOR COMMUNICATION

ADDRESS TO BE WRITTEN HERE

— THIS IS A REAL PHOTOGRAPH —

WITH GREETINGS

## 25

TUCK'S POST CARD

CARTE POSTALE

FOR ADDRESS ONLY

THE WORLD'S ART SERVICE · RAPHAEL TUCK & SONS

TRADE MARK

BY APPOINTMENT FINE ART PUBLISHERS

To bring you greetings

REAL PHOTOGRAPH

Raphael Tuck & Sons Ltd.

ONE SET PUBLISHED TO THEIR MAJESTIES THE KING & QUEEN AND TO HER MAJESTY QUEEN MARY

Printed in England

## 28

POST CARD

PRINTED IN ENGLAND

THIS SPACE FOR COMMUNICATION

ADDRESS TO BE WRITTEN HERE

— THIS IS A REAL PHOTOGRAPH —

With Best Wishes

## 27

POST CARD

SERIES

PRINTED IN GREAT BRITAIN

Address

THIS IS A REAL PHOTOGRAPH

Communication

Published by Lansdowne Production Co., London.

ON THE BALCONY OF BUCKINGHAM PALACE
THE CORONATION OF HER MAJESTY QUEEN ELIZABETH,
JUNE 2ND, 1953

C 33

THE ROYAL HOMECOMING
ON THE BALCONY AT BUCKINGHAM PALACE

H 12

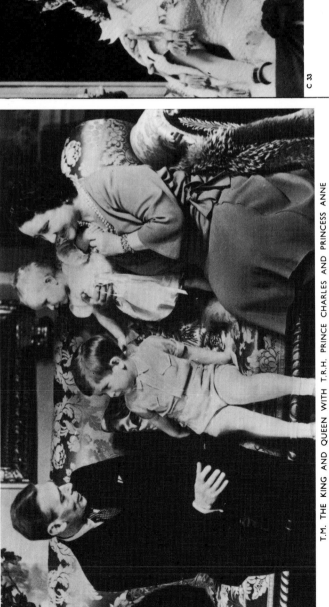

T.M. THE KING AND QUEEN WITH T.R.H. PRINCE CHARLES AND PRINCESS ANNE

Home at last.

THE ROYAL FAMILY AT BALMORAL.

36/1

— THIS IS A REAL PHOTOGRAPH —

POST
GREETINGS

Valentine's

CARD
ADDRESS

---

THE ROYAL FAMILY AT BALMORAL.

36/11

— THIS IS A REAL PHOTOGRAPH —

POST
GREETINGS

Valentine's

CARD
ADDRESS

---

THE ROYAL FAMILY AT BALMORAL.

36/3

— THIS IS A REAL PHOTOGRAPH —

POST
GREETINGS

Valentine's

CARD
ADDRESS

---

THE ROYAL FAMILY AT BALMORAL.

36/7

— THIS IS A REAL PHOTOGRAPH —

POST
GREETINGS

Valentine's

CARD
ADDRESS

HER MAJESTY THE QUEEN WITH H.R.H. PRINCE CHARLES
AND H.R.H. PRINCESS ANNE.

Copyright Marcus Adams. RG.1

*Photochrom Co. Ltd.,*
*Tunbridge Wells, Kent*

Their Royal Highnesses
Prince Charles & Princess Anne

*From a Portrait*
*by Marcus Adams*

129M

Photo : LISA

T.R.H. THE DUKE OF CORNWALL AND PRINCESS ANNE

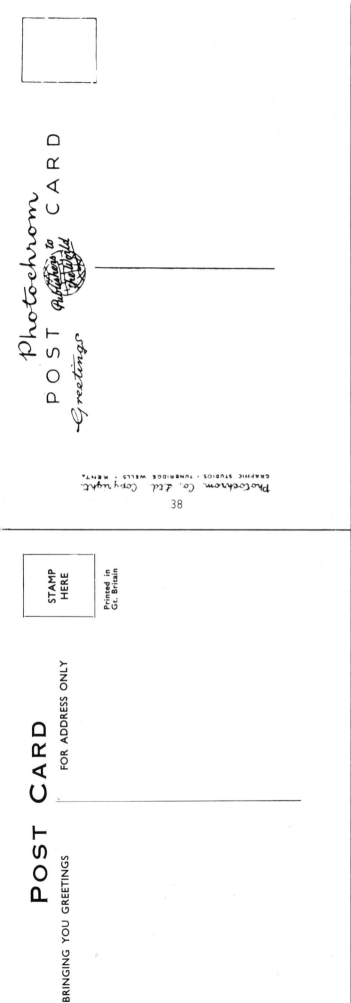

Photochrom
POST CARD
Publishers to the World
Greetings

Photochrom Co. Ltd. Copyright
GRAPHIC STUDIOS · TUNBRIDGE WELLS · KENT.

38

POST CARD
Series
Greetings
Address
PRINTED IN GREAT BRITAIN
THIS IS A REAL PHOTOGRAPH
LANSDOWNE PUBLISHING CO LTD, LONDON

37

POST CARD
FOR ADDRESS ONLY
STAMP HERE
Printed in Gt. Britain
BRINGING YOU GREETINGS
Published by H. A. & W. L. Pitkin Ltd., 9 Northington St., London, W.C.1

40

TUCK'S POST CARD
CARTE POSTALE
TRADE MARK
THE WORLD'S ART SERVICE
FOR ADDRESS ONLY
GREETINGS TO YOU
BY APPOINTMENT FINE ART PUBLISHERS
Printed in England
Raphael Tuck & Sons Ltd.
REAL PHOTOGRAPH
FINE ART PUBLISHERS BY APPOINTMENT TO THE LATE KING GEORGE VI
THE LATE QUEEN MARY AND TO H.M. QUEEN ELIZABETH THE QUEEN MOTHER

39

## Card 42

POST CARD

*L*

Series

PRINTED
IN
GREAT
BRITAIN

Address

Greetings

THIS IS A REAL PHOTOGRAPH

LANSDOWNE PUBLISHING CO LTD., LONDON

42

## Card 41

THE QUEEN'S GALLERY

BUCKINGHAM PALACE

A. K. Lawrence. His Royal Highness Charles, Prince of Wales.
Drawn at Windsor in April 1957.
Printed by B. Matthews (Photo Printers) Ltd., Brighouse, Yorkshire

41

## Card 44

POST *Valentine's* CARD

GREETINGS

ADDRESS

— THIS IS A REAL PHOTOGRAPH —

36/21

H.M. THE QUEEN WITH HER FAMILY IN WINDSOR CASTLE GARDENS.

44

## Card 43

POST CARD

*L*

Series

PRINTED
IN
GREAT
BRITAIN

Address

Greetings

THIS IS A REAL PHOTOGRAPH

LANSDOWNE PUBLISHING CO LTD., LONDON

43

POST

FOR CORRESPONDENCE

*Valentine's*

CARD

ADDRESS

THIS IS A REAL PHOTOGRAPH

THE ROYAL FAMILY AT BALMORAL.    36/24

5099 STYLE U
PRINTED IN GT. BRITAIN

45

POST

FOR CORRESPONDENCE

*Valentine's*

CARD

ADDRESS

THIS IS A REAL PHOTOGRAPH

THE ROYAL FAMILY AT BALMORAL.    36/23

5099 STYLE U
PRINTED IN GT. BRITAIN

46

POST

GREETINGS

*Valentine's*

CARD

ADDRESS

THIS IS A REAL PHOTOGRAPH

H.M. THE QUEEN WITH HER FAMILY IN THE
EAST TERRACE GARDEN, WINDSOR CASTLE.    36/19

47

POST

FOR CORRESPONDENCE

*Valentine's*

CARD

ADDRESS

THIS IS A REAL PHOTOGRAPH

THE ROYAL FAMILY AT BALMORAL.    36/22

5099 STYLE U
PRINTED IN GT. BRITAIN

48

**Card 49:**

VALENTINE'S 'REAL PHOTO'

PUBLISHED BY VALENTINE & SONS LTD., DUNDEE & LONDON

PRINTED IN GT. BRITAIN

Y

H.M. THE QUEEN AND THE DUKE OF EDINBURGH WITH THEIR FAMILY IN THE GROUNDS OF FROGMORE, WINDSOR.

PHOTO BY PRESS ASSOCIATION PHOTOS LTD. X.49

49

**Card 50:**

POST CARD

Printed by B. Matthews (Photo Printers) Ltd., Brighouse, Yorks.
Copyright Reserved

Their Royal Highnesses, The Prince of Wales, Princess Anne, Prince Andrew and Prince Edward, in the garden at Balmoral Castle.

50

**Card 51:**

POST CARD

FOR CORRESPONDENCE

Valentine's

FOR ADDRESS ONLY

PRINTED IN GT. BRITAIN

5099 STYLE W

— THIS IS A REAL PHOTOGRAPH —

AN INFORMAL PHOTOGRAPH OF THE ROYAL FAMILY.
COPYRIGHT ARCHIE PARKER. 36/32

51

**Card 52:**

VALENTINE'S 'REAL PHOTO'

PUBLISHED BY VALENTINE & SONS LTD., DUNDEE & LONDON

PRINTED IN GT. BRITAIN

Y

H.M. THE QUEEN AND THE DUKE OF EDINBURGH WALKING WITH THEIR FAMILY IN THE GROUNDS OF FROGMORE, WINDSOR.

52

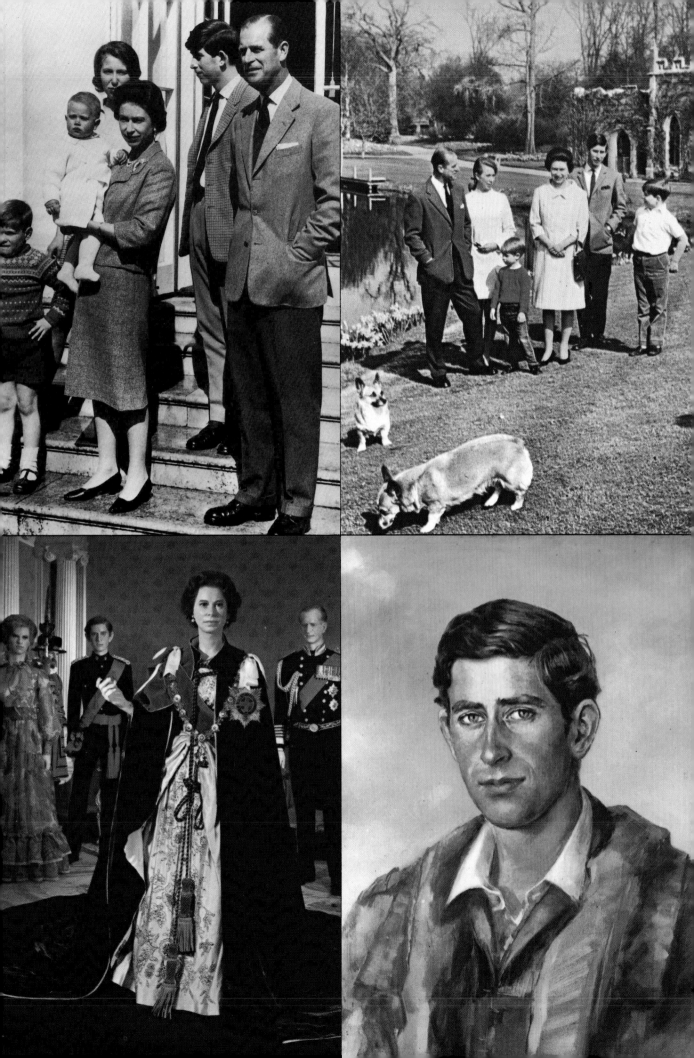

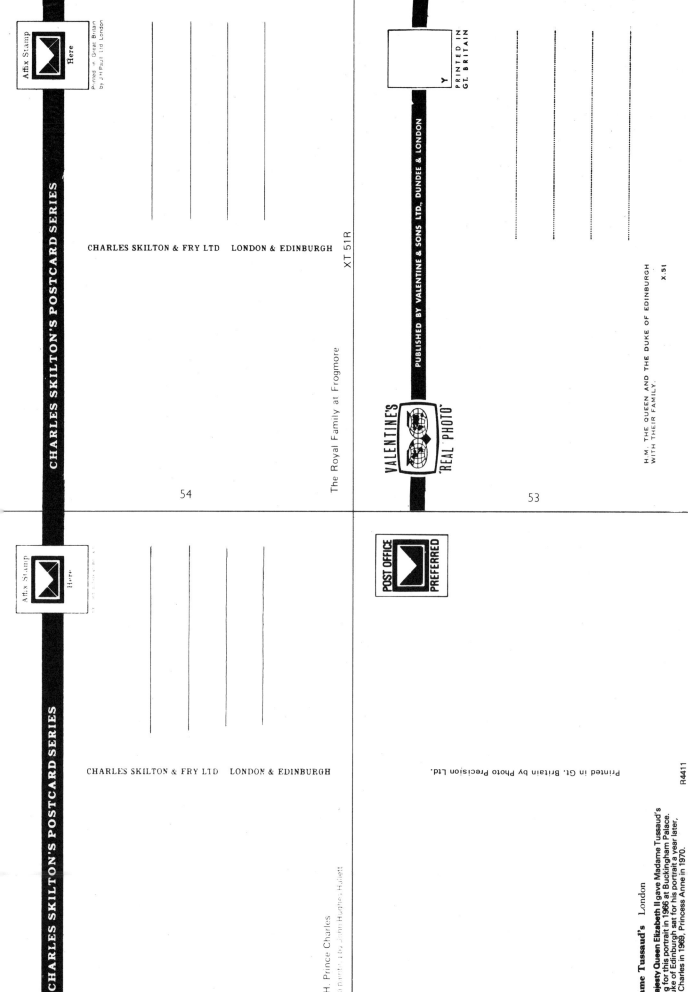

## Card 54

**CHARLES SKILTON'S POSTCARD SERIES**

CHARLES SKILTON & FRY LTD    LONDON & EDINBURGH

XT 51R

The Royal Family at Frogmore

54

## Card 53

PUBLISHED BY VALENTINE & SONS LTD, DUNDEE & LONDON

Y

VALENTINE'S 'REAL PHOTO'

H.M. THE QUEEN AND THE DUKE OF EDINBURGH
WITH THEIR FAMILY.

X.51

53

## Card 56

**CHARLES SKILTON'S POSTCARD SERIES**

CHARLES SKILTON & FRY LTD    LONDON & EDINBURGH

249
H.R.H. Prince Charles
From a photo by John Hughes Hallett

56

## Card 55

POST OFFICE PREFERRED

Printed in Gt. Britain by Photo Precision Ltd.

**Madame Tussaud's**   London

Her Majesty Queen Elizabeth II gave Madame Tussaud's
a sitting for this portrait in 1966 at Buckingham Palace.
The Duke of Edinburgh sat for his portrait a year later,
Prince Charles in 1969, Princess Anne in 1970.

R4411

55

H.R.H. Prince Charles.

XT.53R

Caernarvon Castle.

Buckingham Palace.

Commemorating the investiture of
H.R.H. The Prince of Wales,
Caernarvon Castle,
1st. July 1969

Caernarvon Castle

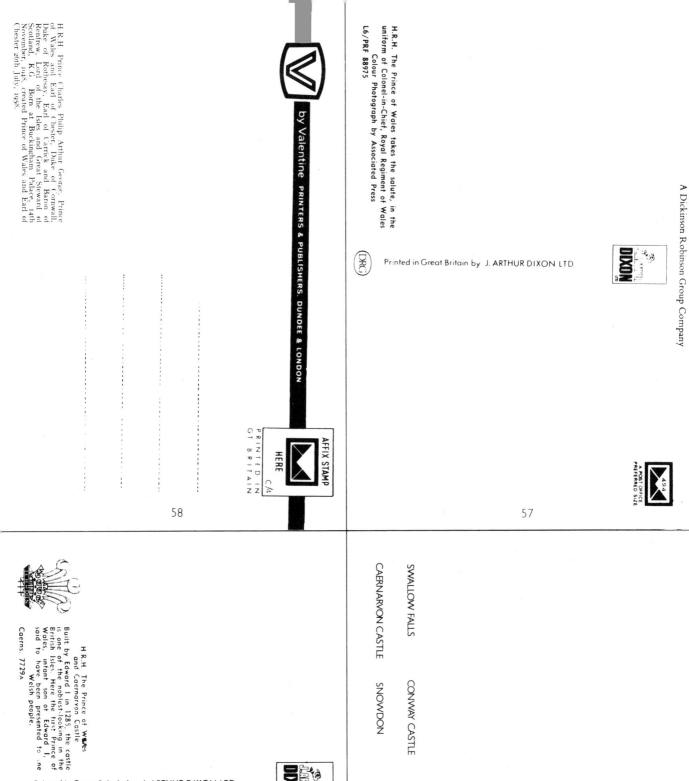

H.R.H. The Prince of Wales takes the salute, in the uniform of Colonel-in-Chief, Royal Regiment of Wales
Colour Photograph by Associated Press

L6/PRF 88975

(DRG) Printed in Great Britain by J. ARTHUR DIXON LTD

A POST OFFICE PREFERRED SIZE 494

57

---

by Valentine PRINTERS, PUBLISHERS, DUNDEE & LONDON

H R H Prince Charles Philip Arthur George, Prince of Wales and Earl of Chester, Duke of Cornwall, Duke of Rothesay, Earl of Carrick and Baron of Renfrew, Lord of the Isles and Great Steward of Scotland, K.G. Born at Buckingham Palace, 14th November, 1948, created Prince of Wales and Earl of Chester 26th July, 1958.

AFFIX STAMP HERE
PRINTED IN GT BRITAIN C/A

58

---

SWALLOW FALLS   CONWAY CASTLE

CAERNARVON CASTLE   SNOWDON   INV2

PRINTED IN GREAT BRITAIN

59

---

H.R.H The Prince of Wales and Caernarvon Castle
Built by Edward I in 1285, the castle is one of the noblest-looking in the British Isles. Here the first Prince of Wales, infant son of Edward I, is said to have been presented to the Welsh people.
Caerns. 7729a.

Printed in Great Britain by J. ARTHUR DIXON LTD.

60

PITKIN PICTORIAL POSTCARDS

Published by Topical Press Ltd 11 Wyfold Road London SW6

H.R.H. PRINCE CHARLES, PRINCE OF WALES

L011/70/10

62

I.C.44.
Investiture of H.R.H. Prince Charles, Prince of Wales,
Caernarfon Castle, 1st July 1969.
H.R.H. Prince Charles, Prince of Wales, 1969.
Arwisgiad Ei Uchelder Brenhinol y Tywysog Charles,
Tywysog Cymru, Castell Caernarfon Gorffennaf 1af,
1969.
Ei Uchelder Brenhinol, y Tywysog Charles, Tywysog
Cymru, 1969.

*Photograph by Norman Parkinson.*

61

COLOURMASTER
INTERNATIONAL

Photo Precision Limited, St. Ives, Huntingdon

This photograph shows H.R.H. The Prince of
Wales on the occasion of the installation of
Knights of the Most Noble Order of the Garter
in June 1972. The Order dates back to 1348.

PT9974

64

CHARLES SKILTON'S POSTCARD SERIES

CHARLES SKILTON & FRY LTD    LONDON & EDINBURGH

His Royal Highness The Prince of Wales as Knight of the Garter
Photographed by Godfrey Argent in the Garter Throne Room at
Windsor Castle.

63

A COTMAN-COLOR SERIES POSTCARD
Printed and Published in Great Britain
by Jarrold & Sons Ltd, Norwich, England

H.R.H. The Prince of Wales
CKBAL 16

66

65

A COTMAN-COLOR SERIES POSTCARD
Printed and Published in Great Britain
by Jarrold & Sons Ltd, Norwich, England

H.R.H. The Prince of Wales

Affix Stamp Here

Printed in Great Britain

Affix Stamp Here

Printed in Great Britain

CHARLES SKILTON'S POSTCARD SERIES

CHARLES SKILTON'S POSTCARD SERIES

CHARLES SKILTON & FRY LTD · 01-840-0404

510

CHARLES SKILTON & FRY LTD

H.R.H. The Prince of Wales wearing the uniform
of a Colonel of the Welsh Guards.
*Photograph by Peter Grugeon.*

68

67

507

H.R.H. The Prince of Wales wearing the uniform of the
Colonel-in-Chief, Royal Regiment of Wales, service dress.

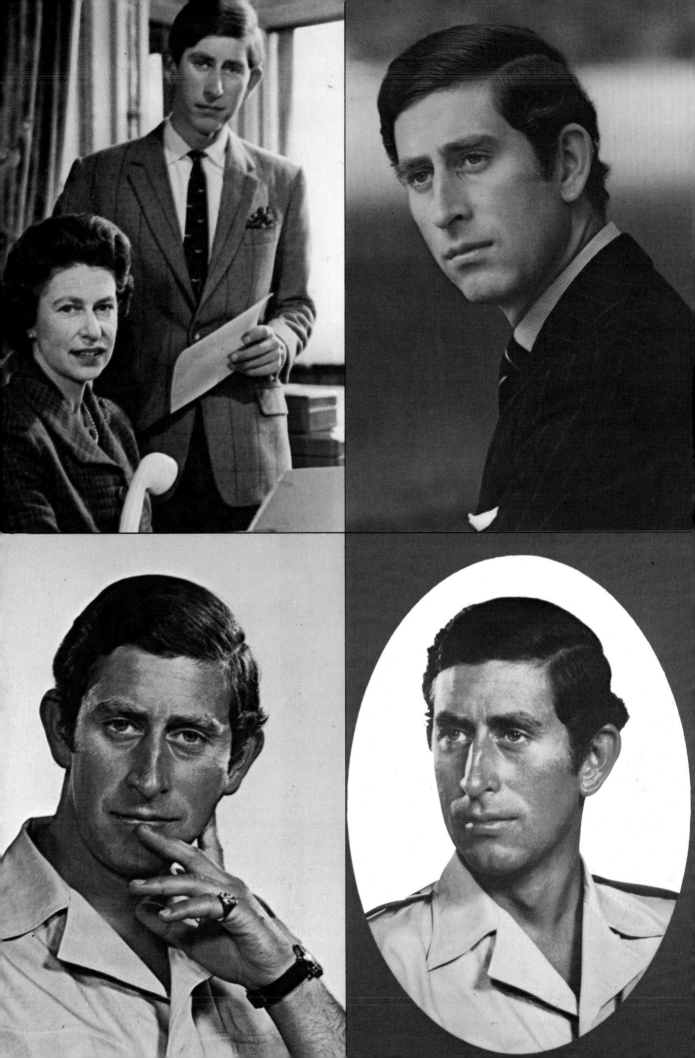

## 70

PITKIN PICTORIAL POSTCARDS

AFFIX STAMP HERE
POST OFFICE PREFERRED

Published by Topical Press Ltd 11 Wyfold Road London SW6

H.R.H. Charles, Prince of Wales
*Photograph by Carole Cutner*

## 69

POST CARD
FROM LONDON

120

THE QUEEN AND PRINCE CHARLES

## 72

*J Arthur Dixon*

A POST OFFICE PREFERRED SIZE

Printed in Great Britain

H.R.H. Prince Charles, The Prince of Wales
Photographed at the residence of the Governor General of Canada in Ottawa; the Prince, a lieutenant in the Royal Navy, took part in NATO exercises in Canada's Arctic Region

*Photograph by KARSH of Ottawa*
Supplied by Camera Press Limited

.PRF/23551

DRG

## 71

CHARLES SKILTON'S POSTCARD SERIES

Affix Stamp Here

Printed in Great Britain

CHARLES SKILTON & FRY LTD

501

H.R.H. The Prince of Wales
Portrait by Karsh, Ottawa

The Royal Wedding Day 29 July 1981

THE ROYAL FAMILY

A COTMAN-COLOR SERIES POSTCARD
Printed and Published in Great Britain
by Jarrold & Sons Ltd, Norwich, England

73

---

Photo Precision Limited,
St. Ives, Huntingdon, Cambs.
Tel: (0480) 64364

The Royal Family at Sandringham in January 1977
CKSH 16

colourmaster international

GS 2513

St. Paul's Cathedral
by night

Buckingham
Palace

The Royal Family

PLX10

POST OFFICE PREFERRED
Printed in Great Britain

74

---

The Royal Family

Photograph by Keystone Press Agency Limited

PRF/23555

Printed in Great Britain by  J. ARTHUR DIXON

DIXON

DRG

A POST OFFICE PREFERRED SIZE
24

76

---

A Dickinson Robinson Group Product

XT.8IR

CHARLES SKILTON & FRY LTD · LONDON & EDINBURGH

CHARLES SKILTON'S POSTCARD SERIES

Affix Stamp Here

Printed in Great Britain
by J H Paull & Co Ltd
London  E 14

75

*The Prince of Wales and Lady Diana Spencer*

Charles and Diana

A COTMAN-COLOR SERIES POSTCARD
Printed and Published in Great Britain
by Jarrold & Sons Ltd, Norwich, England

H.R.H. Prince Charles at Balmoral
*Photograph by Godfrey Argent*
CKBAL 1

78

---

Affix Stamp
Here
Printed in Great Britain

**CHARLES SKILTON'S POSTCARD SERIES**

CHARLES SKILTON & FRY LTD

H.R.H. The Prince of Wales
Prince Charles — bearded after his trek in the
Himalayan foothills, beneath the Annapurna
range, Nepal.

77

---

*Charles and Diana*

A Commemorative Souvenir Postcard by J. Arthur Dixon

Printed in Great Britain

(DRG)

PRF 24957

80

---

POST OFFICE
PREFERRED
Printed in
Great Britain

Colourmaster
International
GS 2471

Photo Precision Limited,
St. Ives, Huntingdon, Cambs.
Tel: (0480) 64364

79